My Emotions Are a Gift

Wisdom from Grandma Series - Book 3

Grace Boucaud-Moore

Illustrated by Amanda Chureson

All rights reserved. No part of this publication may be reproduced, distributed, or transmitted in any form or by any means, including photocopying, recording, or other electronic or mechanical methods, without the prior written permission of the publisher, except in the case of brief quotations embodied in critical reviews and certain other noncommercial uses permitted by copyright law. For permission requests, write to the publisher, TEACH Services, Inc., at the address below.

Copyright © 2023 Grace Boucaud-Moore
Copyright © 2023 TEACH Services, Inc.
ISBN-13: 978-1-4796-1569-8 (Paperback)
ISBN-13: 978-1-4796-1570-4 (ePub)
Library of Congress Control Number: 2022923418

My Emotions Are a Gift

God gave me a body
A body you can see
But wonder of wonders
That isn't all of me

Though my body is remarkable
I have an inner world
My mind's full of imagination
To captivate the soul

God gave us emotions to enable us to enjoy both our physical and spiritual interactions. They spring from our beliefs or perceptions about how others feel about us and treat us and our situations or experiences. Also, how we see ourselves gives rise to emotions. Our right understanding of God, the One who made us and loves us, is enough to sustain healthy emotions because we get our value from Him.

John 4:24; 1 Chronicles 29:18

It has its own affections
Some weaker than the rest
These sometimes cause affliction
And put me to the test

Man's mistake in believing a lie and casting truth aside spoilt his emotional life as well as his physical and spiritual experiences. Without the help of God, his incorrect beliefs and misdirected goals and desires lead man to make bad choices at every turn. Asking for God's strength should be priority.

2 Corinthians 10:5

God sees my expressions
They are reflected in my face
But He knows more about me
Like how much I need His grace

God has not lost sight of mankind. He loves us as much as ever and has provided His many counsels to help us in our difficulties.

Psalm 139:1–4

My feelings come unbidden
I never have to call
They tell me when there's danger
That I could have a fall

God wants to coach us in the proper management of an array of situations and emotional responses. It is not His will that our emotions derail us, but that we identify them and engage them fully for our enjoyment or redemption. As we trace our emotions to their true source (perceptions and beliefs), we will identify whether they are justified or unrighteous and adjust our behaviours as appropriate.

Genesis 4:5–7

Some feelings are quite pleasant
And bring me lots of joy
But others, they are hateful
And make me somewhat coy

While God's Word cheers and comforts those who believe, the cultures of our world bring us unimaginable pain at times. Many live for things and pursue physical pleasure to excess as well as the applause of men. Naturally this leads to competition among ourselves, producing winners and losers.

John 16:33; Romans 8:5

When feelings stir up trouble
Or they feel out of place
I take deep breaths and hear them
And so avoid disgrace

Negative emotions cause pain but it is unwise to ignore them or to lash out because of them. God counsels us to engage in self-talk—question ourselves honestly and remind ourselves that we are not alone and that we have a helper [God].

Psalm 42:11

general lightness

smiley

relaxed muscles

warmth

openness

In time I get the message
And with good friends express
I am thankful for these signals
To pursue true happiness

As we confess our true feelings and related beliefs and goals to God and trustworthy individuals who may be involved, we will be appropriately supported and forgiven.

1 John 1:8–2:2

I name and claim my feelings
And then they get quite tame
You too should name your feelings
And banish every shame

God knows and makes provision for deliverance from our sin condition and the whole human race is acquainted with our innately evil tendencies. Still, it takes humility to confess our self-sufficient attitudes and admit our absolute need for God.

Hebrews 4:15–16; 2:18

The environment around us
Should support us in this way
To make sense of our emotions
And avoid a major fray

The support of others needs to be both accessed and trusted, for it to be effective. Empathy is key to convicting others of our genuine support, but in the case of God, parents must early heed the counsel of Deuteronomy 6 and not give children any reason to doubt their integrity or the integrity of scripture, as competing forces abound in the form of entertaining fictional literature and other sources of instruction.

Psalm 73; Hebrews 11:6

Understanding works like magic
To soothe and not repress
For with acceptance comes
The opportunity for redress

God invites each of us to come and reason with Him without judgment and offers us full acceptance and wisdom to live victoriously.

Isaiah 1:18; James 1:5; Psalm 119:18

When I know just what I am feeling
And what the feeling is for
I can make some changes
So harmful feelings trouble me no more

The Word of God is clear that its purpose is to provide guidance and encouragement and comfort to us as we strive to be pleasing to God.

Ephesians 4: 13–14; 2 Timothy 3:16–17; 1 Peter 5:7–8

Sometimes I play at winning
And other times, I think it best
To consider all my options
And hold a big contest

David and Jacob knew from experience that they could not deliver themselves, but the temptation to try is always present. One way of preparing for success in handling a situation is to walk through it in our minds as a trial run to predict outcomes. Children can do a concrete exercise which nature often guides them to do. However, guardians should encourage prayer and faith-building as exercised by Jacob.

1 Samuel 21:10–15; Genesis 32:11, 22–29

> Once my best of options
> Has surely had its say
> I bend my will to accomplish
> That task in the very best way

Brainstorming solutions that are in line with God's principles gives us options in dealing with life's challenges or dilemmas. However, we will eventually have to make a choice and should avoid procrastinating for too long or we can lose the necessary courage. The biblical Esther is a good example.

Esther 1–10

> I am not afraid of feelings
> They too are a gift, you see
> I cherish and respect them
> As I reflect on me

The scripture assures us that "perfect love casts out fear," meaning that a right relationship to God makes us fearless. With the Holy Spirit as our ally, we are more than conquerors.

Galatians 5:16–24; Luke 15:11–32

tightness of the chest

watery eyes

stinging in the throat

heaviness of the limbs

slouch

A Word to Parents

If you will acquaint them with the relevant vocabulary, children will more readily identify the cues of their emotions and better express their feelings as they seek your support. You can model for them by sharing your emotions and feelings (interoception) or you can use pictures and stories to label emotions and discuss the various situations that may give rise to overwhelming feelings or quiet, pleasant emotions.

Here is a sample "beginner's emotion word bank":

Happy	Sad	Angry	Afraid	Surprised
Embarrassed	Emotions	Name	Claim	Breathe
Focus	Good	Bad	Safe	Inside
Feel	Better	Trust	Think	Pain

You may naturally soothe or comfort the infant by singing, rocking, hugging, or other pleasant distraction, but as they grow and mature, additional support through impartation of language and other problem-solving skills are generally more effective. These include relief solutions like sensing internal feelings (interoception), naming or identification of feelings and emotions, owning or admission of experiences, deep-breathing or blowing, mindful focus, taking a time-out for reflecting, fact-finding, and using helpful resources for self-regulating or co-regulating as necessary.

It will become necessary to increase the "beginner's emotion word bank" by including additional, related words as follows:

Quiet place	Relief	Tense/tight	Calm	Still
Better	Choose	Fist	Stomach	Heart
Knees	Brain/Head	Sweaty	Butterflies	Wobbly/Weak
Belly	Chest	Mouth	Eyes	Jaw
Face	Throbbing	Tingly	Heavy	Knot
Hot	Cold	Shaky		

Soon the child will learn to stop and count or focus mindfully through use of some interoception activity, think about what is upsetting in the given situation, and share their feelings with a trusted friend or adult who can help them co-regulate those overwhelming feelings and impulses. They will also learn to identify those thoughts that can be offensive to others and, therefore, should not be spoken out loud, from those that can and should be freely shared to build positive relationships, or from those that should only be shared with trusted friends and adults. Eventually, they will learn to self-monitor his or her internal feelings to manage their build-up and master the art of expressing feelings and needs respectfully while keeping emotions under control.

GRACE BOUCAUD-MOORE

TEACH Services, Inc.
P U B L I S H I N G

We invite you to view the complete
selection of titles we publish at:
www.TEACHServices.com

We encourage you to write us
with your thoughts about this,
or any other book we publish at:
info@TEACHServices.com

TEACH Services' titles may be purchased in
bulk quantities for educational, fund-raising,
business, or promotional use.
bulksales@TEACHServices.com

Finally, if you are interested in seeing
your own book in print, please contact us at:
publishing@TEACHServices.com
We are happy to review your manuscript at no charge.

www.ingramcontent.com/pod-product-compliance
Lightning Source LLC
Chambersburg PA
CBHW061119170426
43200CB00023B/2994